Getting To Know...

Nature's Children

DEER

Laima Dingwall

PUBLISHER	Joseph R. DeVarennes
PUBLICATION DIRECTOR	Kenneth H. Pearson
MANAGING EDITOR	Valerie Wyatt
SERIES ADVISOR	Merebeth Switzer
SERIES CONSULTANT	Michael Singleton
CONSULTANTS	Ross James
	Kay McKeever
	Dr. Audrey N. Tomera
ADVISORS	Roger Aubin
	Robert Furlonger
	Gaston Lavoie
EDITORIAL SUPERVISOR	Jocelyn Smyth
PRODUCTION MANAGER	Don Markle
PRODUCTION ASSISTANTS	Penelope Moir
	Steve Soloman
EDITORS	Mary Frances Coady — Sarah Reid
	Katherine Farris — Cathy Ripley
	Cristel Kleitsch — Eleanor Tourtel
	Elizabeth MacLeod — Kathy Vanderlinden
	Anne Minguet-Patocka — Karin Velcheff
PHOTO EDITORS	Laurel Haslett
	Pamela Martin
DESIGN	Annette Tatchell
CARTOGRAPHER	Jane Davie
PUBLICATION ADMINISTRATION	Kathy Kishimoto
	Monique Lemonnier
ARTISTS	Marianne Collins — Greg Ruhl
	Pat Ivy — Mary Theberge

This series is approved and recommended
by the Federation of Ontario Naturalists.

Canadian Cataloguing in Publication Data

Dingwall, Laima, 1953-
  Deer

(Getting to know—nature's children)
Includes index.
ISBN 0-7172-1896-1

1. Deer—Juvenile literature. I. Title
II. Series.

QL737.U55D55 1984   j599.73′57   C84-099388-9

Have you ever wondered . . .

What is the first thing that comes to mind when you hear the word "deer"?

Perhaps you think of the magnificent antlers or the swift grace of deer you have seen. Maybe you think of deer-crossing signs on highways warning drivers that a deer might suddenly burst out of the woods into the path of their cars.

Chances are, however, you think of Bambi. Although Walt Disney made the movie "Bambi" many years ago, his little fawn is still one of the first things most people think of when they hear the word "deer."

It is easy to understand why. With his big eyes, sweet face, and his graceful way of moving, Bambi was truly one of the most beautiful animals in the forest.

This is just as true of real deer. And there is a good chance that you have seen a real deer, either in the zoo or in the woods. After all, there are close to 20 million deer in North America.

Meet the Relatives

If the White-tailed Deer held a family reunion for its North American relatives, who would come? Its close cousin, the Mule Deer, of course, and its other cousins, the elk, moose and caribou.

All these members of the deer family have a number of things in common. For instance, they all chew cud, none has any top front teeth, and they all have split hoofs for feet.

Of course, some or even all these things are true of other animals as well. But the members of the deer family have one more thing in common: the males all grow and shed a set of antlers each year. This is what makes them different from all other animals.

White-Tailed Deer Country

There are about 14 million White-tailed Deer in North America. They are found right across the central and southern parts of the continent except in the high mountains and deserts of the far West.

Look for White-tailed Deer near clearings around forests, on the edges of swamps and glades, near the banks of streams and ponds, and close to farmland. These are the places where the deer can find the plants, shrubs and small trees that it needs for food and protection.

Where deer are found in North America

Deer Up Close

There are about 30 varieties of White-tailed Deer in North America. Most are quite similar in appearance and manners. In fact, it is often difficult to tell them apart—except, in some cases, for size.

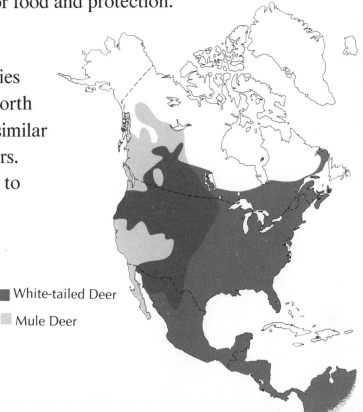

■ White-tailed Deer

■ Mule Deer

A large body loses heat less quickly than a small one. For this reason, the farther north, and the colder the climate in which the deer live, the larger they will tend to be. In more northern regions, a full-grown male, called a buck, stands just under a metre (38 inches) tall from his hoofs to his shoulders. He weighs more than most adult men. The female, called a doe, is slightly smaller. In the South, in places such as Florida, deer are barely more than half the size.

In summer a deer has a short, reddish-brown coat made of stiff, wiry hairs. It starts getting ready for winter in late August by replacing its summer coat with a thick, gray-blue winter one. The hairs in this coat are long and hollow. They trap the air warmed by the deer's body heat and help keep the deer cozy even in the coldest weather. In winter, the deer also has an under-coat of downy hairs to give extra warmth.

Deer tend to be larger the farther north they live. However a deer will grow bigger if it eats good food.

The Mule Deer

Next to the White-tailed Deer, the most common deer in North America is the Mule Deer. It lives in the open forests, brush and parklands of western North America.

You can tell the Mule Deer from the White-tailed Deer in four ways.

First, the antlers of Mule bucks branch in pairs rather than singly. The second thing you notice is that the Mule Deer's ears are huge. In fact, this deer got its name because its big ears reminded people of a mule's ears. The Mule Deer also has an unusual way of moving. When it bounds, it keeps its legs very stiff and its four feet touch the ground at the same time. Last, but not least, the Mule Deer has a short black-tipped tail which, unlike the white-tailed deer, it does not flip up and wave like a flag.

Antlers

White-tailed Deer

Mule Deer

A Rack of Antlers

Imagine carrying a rack of antlers as wide as your outstretched arms and as heavy as a bag of potatoes on your head. That is the size of antlers on the average full-grown buck.

Only male deer grow antlers, and they grow new set every year. They use them mainly to fight for mates.

Antlers start to develop in spring. While they are growing, they are covered with a thick, soft skin called velvet. This skin contains the blood vessels that nourish the antlers and make them grow.

By late summer, the antlers are full grown, and the velvety skin starts to dry up and peel off. This can make the deer look very messy. But not for long—the deer helps get rid of the strips of hanging velvet by rubbing his antlers against trees.

Antlers usually fall off one at a time in winter—often in mid-December. They break free near the deer's head. A deer may have red sores in those spots for a few days, but these soon heal.

Opposite page:

Buck in January. The magnificent antlers have fallen off and it will be many weeks before a new set starts to grow.

15

Once the antlers are on the ground, little creatures like mice and chipmunks are quick to come and nibble at them. Antlers are full of calcium and other minerals that are good for these little animals.

Big, Bigger, Biggest

A buck will probably grow his first set of antlers during the second summer of his life. Often these will just be smooth, straight spikes, about 12-13 centimetres (5 inches) long. Where good food is plentiful, however, these first antlers may develop several branches or points. By the time a buck is four or five years old, his antlers will usually have about eight points, though many more can grow.

Some people think you can tell how old a buck is by the size of his antlers or by the number of points they grow. This is not true. Once a buck is full-grown—at age four or so—the size of his antlers depends mainly on how healthy he is. A deer that is getting lots of good food to eat will usually grow the biggest set of antlers.

Bucks use their antlers mainly to fight for mates. The fights are seldom really serious—more like a shoving match. One buck, probably the smaller, will usually back away before anyone gets hurt.

Seeing, Smelling and Hearing

If you were to put on your brightest red sweater and stand very still in front of a deer, it might not even notice you. That is because deer are color blind. Those big, soft brown eyes see the world in shades of gray—a little like watching a black and white television set. To the deer, you would be just another grayish pattern in the forest. But move—even just blink your eye—and a deer, with its excellent ability to spot movement, will see you.

And if you are thinking of trying to sneak up on a deer from behind, don't bother unless the wind is blowing in the right direction. A deer has a very keen sense of smell. If the wind is carrying your scent its way, the deer will pick it up and be gone long before you can get near.

Deer are timid creatures. They cannot defend themselves very effectively if attacked and so will take off at the first sign of danger.

If you are downwind, the deer will not be able to smell you. But you will still not find it easy to get near, for the deer also has a sharp sense of hearing. When a deer cocks up its pointy ears, it can hear sounds long before you can. The first strange sound might not send it fleeing, but a second or a third will send it bounding away.

Deer on the Move

Watch a deer bound and you would swear it had springs in its legs. First, its two front legs touch the ground at the same time, then its two back legs touch down. It takes three short bounds then one big l-e-a-p that can cover a distance about the length of a van.

A deer can gallop as fast as a horse over short distances, and even a pile of rocks or a fence will not slow it down. It can clear obstacles three metres (10 feet) high, or about the height of two medium-sized cars stacked on top of one another.

Deer Tracks

Buck

Doe

Fawn

If there is a pond in the deer's path, that is no problem either. Instead of changing direction, a deer is just as likely to leap right into the water and swim across. Deer are good swimmers. During the late spring and summer, deer often wade neck-deep into nearby lakes to get away from pesky black flies and mosquitoes.

A deer's hoofs give it a good grip when it is running on hard ground. But on ice they slip and slide. Also, their sharp hoofs, not made for running on top of deep snow, sink down and prevent the deer from moving quickly. So getting around in winter can be a problem.

It is easy to see why deep snow is a serious problem for deer.

Opposite page:
Although deer tend to stay within a fairly small territory, they sometimes have to travel many miles to find good winter range.

The Deer's Home

It may seem surprising, since they are such good runners, but deer are real homebodies. They do not travel far from their territory unless there is a shortage of food. A deer's territory—the area it considers "home"—is often no bigger than two to three square kilometres (about one square mile). Up to 30 or more adult deer can share a territory this size in an area where there is lots of food.

Within its territory, a deer does not build a nest or even a den like some other animals. Instead, it rests in any place that looks safe and comfortable. That is often on dry, smooth ground surrounded by trees. In winter, a deer often picks a sheltered spot under low-hanging evergreen branches. But wherever it beds down, a deer makes sure that it is not too far from a feeding spot.

26

Dinner Time

Do not ask a deer to smile. That is because it does not have any top front teeth. Instead it has a tough pad that is used for tearing plants and twigs. But to chew its food, a deer has 32 teeth in the rest of its mouth.

What do deer eat? It depends on the season. In spring and summer, grass, plants and weeds top the list, followed closely by tender twigs, buds and leaves from shrubs and trees. In fall, they add acorns and mushrooms to their menu. Apples are favorite treats, and deer will even rear up on their hind legs to reach into a tree to munch on one of these sweet, juicy fruits.

Deer eat a lot—about seven kilograms (15 pounds) on a good summer day.

You can tell a branch chewed by a deer by its ragged end. Since deer have no top front teeth they tear rather than cut cleanly.

Eat Now Chew Later

Deer usually feed in the early morning and again in the evening. They keep moving around as they eat and do not waste much time chewing. That is because, like cows, deer are cud chewers.

Spring at last—Velvet-covered antlers are growing, and a rich supply of juicy twigs and buds will soon fatten up this young Mule buck.

Being a cud chewer means that a deer can eat first and chew later. It has a special part of its stomach where it collects unchewed food. Then it looks for a resting spot that is safe from enemies and out of the hot sun or cold winter winds. There it brings the food, or cud, back to its mouth and chews it in peace. Deer usually lie down to chew—maybe because it is such tiring work. After all, they give each lemon-sized cud about 40 good chews.

Winter Feeding

Unlike squirrels and some other animals, deer do not store food for winter. Instead, they eat what they can find. If there is only a little snow on the ground, deer uncover moss, leaves and even acorns with their hoofs. If the snow is deep and covers up food of this kind, they will eat branches and twigs from trees such as birch, willow, cedar and other evergreens. And if a deer cannot find enough twigs or branches, it will strip bark from trees and eat that.

Deer usually eat facing into the wind so that they have a better chance of catching any strange scent.

Deer find it very tiring to trudge through snow looking for food. So in winter, in northern areas, groups of deer gather together in one place that provides food and shelter from the wind. This activity is called "yarding." The presence of many deer means that the snow gets tramped down and they can move around more easily. If food within the yard runs out, they also tramp down trails or runways that lead to feeding spots beyond.

Danger!

Deer have many enemies. At one time the wolf and the cougar were the main predators of the deer. Today there are fewer of these animals left in the deer's range, and they are not as great a threat as they once were.

Dogs are now near the top of the enemy list. They are especially a danger in winter, when deer have trouble running on ice and through the snow.

A deer's main defences are its speed and its keen senses. Except in winter, a deer can usually outrun its enemies, and it is constantly alert for

any sound, smell or movement that might spell danger. A deer is also on the watch for warnings that might come from the behavior of other deer.

Deer Warnings

If you walk through the woods and hear what sounds like a big sneeze, you might have come close to a deer and not even known it. When a deer is startled or nervous, it blows through its nose, making a snorty, sneezy sound. This clears the deer's nose and helps it sniff the air better. The noise may alert other deer, and it may be so loud that it even frightens away an enemy.

When alarmed, a deer might also thump the ground with its two front feet, as though playing a drum. This too warns other deer that danger is close by.

And a White-tailed Deer in full flight flips up its tail, showing off the pure white fur underneath. This white tail acts as a warning flag. When they see it, other deer heed the warning instantly and dash away, white tails flashing.

A Baby is Born

Deer mate in the fall—usually in mid-November—and by late spring, the doe is ready to give birth. She sometimes picks a quiet spot in the shrubs as a nursery, but often her babies are born by the edge of a field where she has been nibbling grass.

A doe usually has one or two babies, called fawns. Sometimes three babies are born at the same time.

A newborn fawn weighs much the same as you did when you were born—about 3 kilograms (6-7 pounds). But unlike a human baby, a fawn can stand up by itself and even take a few wobbly steps on its long, spindly legs within an hour after it is born.

Even so, a fawn is still weak and helpless. Its mother leads it to a safe spot in shrubs or tall grass where it will be well hidden from predators. If a doe has two fawns, she hides each of them in a different place.

Built-in Protection

The fawn has a reddish-brown coat like its mother's—except for one important difference. The fawn's back is sprinkled with white spots—about 300 of them—each about the size of a quarter. These spots help protect the fawn from enemies. When the fawn lies quietly in the bushes with its legs folded under its body and its chin flat on the ground, its enemies will see what looks like splashes of sunlight on the ground. Even a sharp-eyed eagle flying over-head will be fooled by the fawn's spots and pass right by.

Besides not being able to see the fawn, its enemies will not be able to smell it either. For almost a week after it is born a fawn does not give off any scent. The doe may help get rid of any tell-tale smell by giving her baby a head-to-toe bath with her rough tongue as soon as it is born. Sometimes she is so earnest in her cleaning and may lick it so hard that she knocks her baby off its feet.

Lying perfectly still, its spotted coat blending into the pattern of light and shadow around it, this young fawn is quite well hidden from predators.

A Good Mother

The doe raises her family alone. The buck plays no part in looking after the young.

Once the doe hides her baby she goes off to feed or rest nearby. She does not stay right beside her fawn because her scent would attract enemies. But she stays close enough to sniff the air for any dangerous scents and to listen for any bleats from her hungry fawn.

Sometimes when people find a fawn alone in the woods they think it is an orphan or that it has been abandoned by its mother. That is not true. The mother is close by even though people cannot see her.

First Outings

By the time the fawn is three weeks old, it has doubled its birth weight and is strong enough to follow its mother on her daily outings. At this age, a fawn is fast enough to outrun the average adult man.

It is easy for a fawn to wander away from its mother on these outings. But a doe will be able to find her fawn simply by using her nose. A deer has special glands in its hoofs that leave behind a scent trail when it walks. A mother doe will recognize her own fawn's scent and follow its path to her lost baby.

Even though the fawn is still taking its mother's milk, it is soon beginning to nibble grass, dandelions and tender leaves. Sometimes it even eats some of the leaves sticking out from the corners of its mother's mouth. When the time comes to take a first sip of water, a fawn might test-dip its nose in the pond several times before it finally takes a drink. Before long, it will be drinking about two litres (quarts) of water each day.

Frisky Fawns

With all this eating and drinking, the fawn grows quickly. By the time it is two months old, it weighs as much as a four-year old child. And in just another two months, it will be nearly as big as its mother. By then the fawn will have stopped taking its mother's milk and will be losing its white spots as its winter coat begins to grow.

Fawns seem to enjoy playing. They bound after their mother and chase grasshoppers and butterflies. Sometimes two fawns play a deer's version of leap frog and jump over one another in turn. If there is a pond nearby, a fawn might hop in and splash up and down on all fours in the shallow water.

Finding out about the world under Mom's watchful eye.

Growing Up

All this frisking and frolicking is fun, but it is more than that. The fawns are developing strength, agility and speed. And they are watching their mother and learning, from her example, to recognize signs of danger.

The fawns stay with their mother through their first winter. By spring, they are ready to cope with the world on their own. The young bucks will probably not mate for a year or two, until they are stronger and have grown bigger antlers. Most of the young does, however, will mate in the fall and will have their first babies the following spring.

Special Words

Antlers   Hard, bony growths on the head of male deer.

Blood vessels   Tubes, arteries and veins through which blood flows in the body.

Buck   Male deer.

Cud   Hastily swallowed food brought back for chewing by cud chewers like cows and deer.

Den   Animal home.

Doe   Female deer.

Fawn   Baby deer.

Glade   An open space in a forest.

Hoofs   Feet of deer, cattle and some other animals.

Mate   To come together to produce young.

Predators   Animal that lives by hunting others for food.

Swamp   Area where ground is soaked with water.

Territory: Area that an animal or group of animals lives in and often defends from other animals of the same kind.

Velvet   Soft skin which covers a deer's antlers while they grow.

Yarding   The gathering together of deer for the winter in an area where food and shelter are available.

INDEX

Cover Photo: S.J. Krasemann/Valan Photos
Photo Credits: Norman Lightfoot: pages 4, 7, 8, 11, 14, 16, 25, 27, 37, 42: Lowry Photo: 13, 33; Network Stock Photo File: 21 (Brian Morin); Ontario Ministry of Natural Resources: 22, 30, 34, 45; V. Claerhaut: 28; National Museum of Natural Sciences, Neg. # S79-3275; National Museums of Canada: 38; Parks Canada: 40-41 (W. Wyett).

Getting To Know...

Nature's Children

RABBITS

Merebeth Switzer

PUBLISHER	Joseph R. DeVarennes
PUBLICATION DIRECTOR	Kenneth H. Pearson
MANAGING EDITOR	Valerie Wyatt
SERIES ADVISOR	Merebeth Switzer
SERIES CONSULTANT	Michael Singleton
CONSULTANTS	Ross James
	Kay McKeever
	Dr. Audrey N. Tomera
ADVISORS	Roger Aubin
	Robert Furlonger
	Gaston Lavoie
EDITORIAL SUPERVISOR	Jocelyn Smyth
PRODUCTION MANAGER	Don Markle
PRODUCTION ASSISTANTS	Penelope Moir
	Steve Soloman
EDITORS	Mary Frances Coady	Sarah Reid
	Katherine Farris	Cathy Ripley
	Cristel Kleitsch	Eleanor Tourtel
	Elizabeth MacLeod	Kathy Vanderlinden
	Anne Minguet-Patocka	Karin Velcheff
PHOTO EDITORS	Laurel Haslett
	Pamela Martin
DESIGN	Annette Tatchell
CARTOGRAPHER	Jane Davie
PUBLICATION ADMINISTRATION	Kathy Kishimoto
	Monique Lemonnier
ARTISTS	Marianne Collins	Greg Ruhl
	Pat Ivy	Mary Theberge

This series is approved and recommended
by the Federation of Ontario Naturalists.

Canadian Cataloguing in Publication Data

Switzer, Merebeth.
  Rabbits and hares

(Getting to know—nature's children)
Includes index.
ISBN 0-7172-1895-3

1. Rabbits—Juvenile literature. 2. Hares-
Juvenile literature. I. Title. II. Series.

QL737.L32S87 1984   j599.32'2   C84-099387-0

Have you ever wondered . . .

We all know something about rabbits and hares, even if it is only from watching or reading the adventures of Bugs Bunny or Peter Rabbit.

We know that they all have big ears and short fluffy tails and that they hop. And most of them seem to get into trouble by stealing garden vegetables.

You can probably think of many other story-book rabbits and hares. There is the March Hare in *Alice in Wonderland*, for instance, and that show-off who got taught a valuable lesson in Aesop's fable, *The Hare and the Tortoise*. And of course there is the Easter Bunny.

Certainly these story-book rabbits and hares are delightful and fascinating. But, they are no more fascinating than the real rabbits and hares that roam our fields and woodlands.

Rabbit
38-45 cm (15-18 in)
0.6-1.8 kg (1½-4 lb)

Hare
45-75 cm (18-30 in)
1.8 kg (4 lb)

Rabbits or Hares: Who's Who?

Rabbits and hares are really quite different. But they look very much alike, and it is easy to get confused. In fact, it is so easy to get confused that some of them have been given the wrong names. For example, the Jackrabbit is actually a hare, and the Belgian Hare is actually a rabbit!

So how do you tell them apart? Well, generally, rabbits are much smaller than hares and have shorter legs and ears. But this is not always the case.

The only sure way to tell a rabbit from a hare is to get a look at the newborn babies. Baby hares are born with open eyes and a full covering of fur, and they can hop a few hours after birth. Baby rabbits are born helpless, blind, and with no fur on their bodies. It will be about a week before their eyes open and nearly another week before they are fully furred and hopping around.

Some rabbits and hares may be hard to tell apart, but there is no mistaking the Snowshoe Hare. Its huge, furry hind foot is more than one quarter the length of its body.

Rabbits, Rabbits Everywhere

Rabbits and hares are found all over the world except in Antarctica and the islands of southeast Asia. In some countries, such as Australia, there were no rabbits until fairly recent times. Early settlers brought some with them, and they quickly spread across the land.

In North America, rabbits and hares live in every type of wild area. Hares can live on the cold open tundra of the Arctic, in the hot desert, and high up in the Rocky Mountains. You can find rabbits in fields, swamps, marshes, woods, and even in the parks of big cities. If you live in the country or in a small town, you may very well have seen a rabbit or two in your garden.

All rabbits in North America are Cottontails, but there are several types of hares. The best

Where Cottontail Rabbits are found in North America.

Mother and baby Arctic Hare feast on the many kinds of plants that spring to life on the tundra during the short Arctic summer.

known are the Arctic Hare, the Snowshoe or Varying Hare and the Jackrabbit.

Home is Where You Find It

The hare does not have what we think of as a home. It simply uses whatever hiding place is available. This may be a clump of grass, a hollow log, or the low, overhanging branches of a fir tree. The hare will rest there all day with its body snuggled into the ground. This makes a shallow hollow called a form. A hare may use several forms, but it will usually have a favorite one that is "home."

In the winter, some hares may tunnel a short way into the snow and scratch out a cozy nook to shelter in.

Home to a Snowshoe Hare is often a low-hanging evergreen branch that shelters it from wind and falling snow.

Just as people around the world are different from each other, so are rabbits and hares. In Europe, rabbits build burrows and live in large underground communities called warrens. North American rabbits, on the other hand, follow the hare's example and use forms for sleeping. No one knows why North American rabbits do not dig burrows. It is not that they dislike them, because they do occasionally borrow someone else's—usually a woodchuck's or a skunk's.

Like many "rules" in nature, however, this one has an exception. One kind of Cottontail, the tiny Pygmy Rabbit that lives in the southwestern United States, does dig its own burrow.

A nook in a snowbank might not suit everyone, but it's really quite comfortable—if you're a hare.

Getting Along with Each Other

Rabbits, Jackrabbits and Snowshoe Hares will usually live alone. Jackrabbits, in fact, seldom mix at all, even with their own kind. The others, however, are quite friendly with their close relatives and are sometimes seen feeding together or playing tag in a moonlit field.

On the other hand, the northern Snowshoe Hares and Arctic Hares are often found in large groups of over 100 animals. In these groups, aunts, uncles, brothers and sisters share the same feeding grounds and they will often play together in mock battles and chasing games.

Although both rabbits and hares are friendly towards their own kind, they are not friendly towards each other and you will rarely find rabbits and hares together in the wild.

Dinner-time

Rabbits and hares are most active at night. They spend the day in their forms snoozing and grooming themselves by licking their fur. Then, when it begins to get dark, they come out to look for food. It is safer for them to move around and feed when they cannot be seen.

Rabbits and hares are herbivores. This means they are animals that eat mostly plants. There is nothing a rabbit likes better than fresh greens, and it does not care where it finds them. No wonder farmers and gardeners sometimes think they are pests!

Rabbits and hares are active all year, always searching for food. During the northern winter, they feed on twigs, buds and the bark of certain trees. In the Arctic, where everything is covered by snow most of the time, the hares dig down to get buried moss and plants called lichen (pronounced *like'en*). Arctic Hares need up to half a kilogram (a pound) of food per day. Sometimes, in order to survive the Arctic winter, they will eat meat if they find it.

Better Than a Knife and Fork

Rabbits and hares have a set of very special front teeth to help them snip off plants and twigs for their dinner. Kangaroos can hop, and elephants have big ears, but no other animal has teeth quite like those of our friends the rabbit and hare.

Other animals—squirrels, for instance—have two big front upper teeth for cutting, just as rabbits and hares do. But rabbits and hares have an extra pair of smaller, very sharp front teeth just behind the big ones. This extra pair of cutting teeth is one of the main features that makes rabbits and hares different from all other animals.

Now that looks tender and juicy! What more could a hungry Desert Cottontail ask for?

Too fast for the photographer's camera to catch clearly, this super-hopper can still be identified by the white powder-puff tail that gives it its name.

Getting Around

You know that rabbits and hares do not walk. But do you know what truly champion hoppers they are? If a Snowshoe Hare were as big as you, it would win all the gold medals in high jumping and broad jumping! This hare can jump four and a half metres (15 feet) straight up and can cover a distance about ten times its own length in one hop.

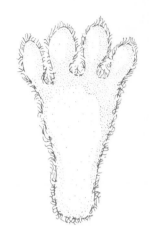

Snowshoe Hare's hind foot.

They are fast hoppers, too. Hares have been recorded at nearly 80 kilometres (50 miles) per hour over short distances. That is the speed cars go on the highways! Rabbits can reach about half that speed.

Jackrabbit's hind foot.

21

How can a rabbit or hare jump that far, that high, and that fast? The secret is in its powerful back legs—they are huge and full of muscles. No wonder the hare in Aesop's fable did not worry about the tortoise in their race!

There is one type of rabbit that not only hops, it swims and even dives underwater. The Marsh or Swamp Rabbit is a type of Cottontail found in the southeastern United States. It gets its name because it likes to live in wet places. On very hot summer days, these rabbits are even seen lolling about in ponds or puddles to keep cool.

Although they move fast, rabbits and hares seldom go very far. Most, in fact, spend their entire lives within 400 metres (1300 feet) of their homes. The Jackrabbit may roam twice as far, however, and all will venture beyond their usual range if food is scarce. At mating season, as well, males may go courting outside their home range.

Snowshoe Hare tracks in snow.

The hour after sunset is a favorite feeding time for bunnies.

Starting a Family

Baby rabbits and hares are born in the spring and summer, when the weather is warm enough for them to survive.

When the first signs of spring appear, the adult rabbits and hares begin their mating season. The males, called bucks, fight each other to decide who will father the young, while the female, the doe, waits nearby. Once this is settled, there may be an elaborate courting dance, with the buck chasing the doe and flagging his tail. The two may then dance around each other, play-box and leap high in the air. Sometimes they will groom each other by licking and nuzzling.

Rabbit Families

In southern Canada and in the northern United States, a doe rabbit may have three to five families, or litters, between March and September. In warmer climates she may have even more.

About four weeks after mating, the doe gets ready for the birth. She makes a nest in a shallow hole in the ground and carefully lines it with soft grasses and plants. She adds pieces of fur plucked from her own coat to make the nest extra warm for her babies. The nest is small and will only have room enough for the young babies, called kits.

Crouching over the nest, the doe gives birth to a litter of five or six babies. The kits are tiny—only about eight centimetres (3 inches) long. They cannot see and are completely helpless at this stage. Shortly after the birth, the mother allows her babies to nurse. Then,

These baby rabbits are probably about a week old. Their eyes are open, their furry coat is growing, and in a few days they will be up on their feet.

to protect the kits, she covers the nest with pieces of plants and she moves a distance away.

Keeping the Babies Safe.
During the first two weeks, the doe leaves the kits alone except when it is time for them to nurse. Even then, she approaches the nest in a careful zigzag pattern and leaps the last few feet in order not to leave a trail. In this way she keeps the babies' hiding place a secret from any animals that might be nearby.

In their nest, the kits are safe from most wild animals. But their open nursery can sometimes place them in danger at the hands of well-meaning people. A person who finds a nest often thinks that the mother has abandoned her babies. Nothing is further from the truth! The mother is very near, and she is looking after her family in the best possible way. Baby rabbits are difficult to care for, and they are safest if left alone.

There is nothing like a nice soft pillow!

Hare Families

Hares usually have fewer litters than rabbits do, and the litters are smaller in size. The mother hare behaves differently from the mother rabbit. She does not make a nest but simply stops at the nearest sheltered spot when she is ready to give birth. The chipmunk-sized babies, called leverets, are born covered in warm fur. Although they can see and are able to hop around a few hours after birth, the leverets still need their mother's care.

Sleeping is what baby Arctic Hares—like baby humans—do best.

The doe nurses her babies once a day under cover of darkness. This is her way of keeping their hiding spot safe from other animals. Like the rabbit, she leaves them alone the rest of the time but remains nearby, ready to lead enemies away. While their mother is gone, the babies huddle together in a warm brown heap for protection. Luckily they can soon scamper away to hide if any danger comes near.

The kits and leverets grow very quickly. Leverets are ready to leave the nest at three weeks, and the kits, who have more growing up to do, leave home at five or six weeks. Brothers and sisters may stay together for a few weeks before going their separate ways.

A baby Snowshoe Hare blends in so well with its surroundings that it is hard to tell where baby stops and surroundings begin.

Jackrabbits

Jackrabbits are actually very long-legged, long-eared hares. There are three main types of Jackrabbits: the Black-tailed Jackrabbit, the White-tailed Jackrabbit and the giant-eared Antelope Jackrabbit. You can guess how the first two got their names, but what about the third? The Antelope Jackrabbit is named for its white rump which looks like the rump of the Pronghorn or American "Antelope."

The Jackrabbit's huge ears are super scopes for sound, but they also serve another purpose: they help to keep the hares body cool in summer. The blood passes out into the ears and is cooled by breezes blowing over them. This helps to cool the whole body.

Where Jackrabbits are found in North America.

A Jackrabbit has the biggest ears for its size of any animal in the world.

The Snowshoe or Varying Hare

This hare lives in the forest. The name "snowshoe" refers to its very large hind feet. These act like built-in snowshoes and help the hare to move over deep snow without sinking up to its furry nose. They are even better than regular snowshoes because they are covered with thick, bristly fur that helps to keep the four big toes on each foot warm.

Where Snowshoe Hares are found in North America.

The Snowshoe or Varying Hare has a long, thick white coat in the winter to keep it warm and act as a disguise. In the spring it sheds this coat and grows a brown summer coat. The new hair is shorter and thinner and helps the hare to hide among the green and brown shadows of the forest. The change from white to brown takes nearly ten weeks, and the hare will look quite splotchy during this time.

Snowshoe Hares often create a year round trail or runway through heavy brush. The runways lead between favorite feeding and resting spots, and they are often borrowed by squirrels, porcupines, skunks, and other animals.

The Arctic Hare

The Arctic Hare is like the Snowshoe Hare, but is is nearly three times as big. A large body keeps warmer than a small one and takes longer to cool down in the cold. This hare also has unusually short ears and legs. The shorter ears and legs are closer to the hare's body and help to keep it warmer. They do not allow the body to cool the way the long legs and ears of the Jackrabbits do.

Where Arctic Hares are found in North America.

The Arctic Hare has a special fur coat made of two layers. Long silky fur lies over a layer of shorter woolly fur next to the body. The top layer keeps out the wind, and the bottom layer supplies warmth.

To save energy, the Arctic Hare spends much of its time sitting very still, like a statue. It tucks its tail and paws under its body and flattens

its ears along its back. It will sit this way sheltered behind rocks and snowdrifts or in the open facing into the wind. The wind presses the fur tightly against the hare's body, which helps to keep in the heat.

In the Southern part of their range, Arctic Hares grow a new brownish coat for summer. In the northern Arctic, however, summer is only a few weeks long, and hares living there do not change their white coats. This makes them very visible in summer against the brown tundra.

The short summer throughout the part of the world in which we find the Arctic Hare allows for only one litter of three to six babies each year. The leverets are greyish-brown at birth, which allows them to blend into their surroundings.

Their white coats make these northern Arctic Hares very easy to spot against the brown of the summer tundra.

A Dangerous Life

Rabbits and most hares have many babies each year. From one summer to the next, two pairs of rabbits could produce more than 160 children and 3000 grandchildren. Now that's a lot of rabbits!

If all the rabbits and hares survived, we would be knee-deep in bunnies. Why doesn't this happen? Small animals, such as rabbits, are very important to the balance of nature. They are dinner to foxes, owls, coyotes, weasels, lynx and others.

With so many animals looking for a meal, rabbits and hares must use all their wits to survive. They are always alert for danger, even when they take a short nap. Their huge ears catch every sound, and their constantly twitching nose sniffs the air for danger. Through the ground they feel the vibrations caused by people or other animals passing by.

Snowshoe Hare in the midst of changing from its white winter coat to its brown summer coat. The change helps protect the hare from its enemies by making it harder to see.

Survival Tricks

If an intruder moves near, rabbits and hares will flatten their ears and crouch close to the ground. If the danger comes nearer still, they flatten their body even further. In this position they look like a small rock.

When it appears that there is no escape from discovery, the rabbit or hare explodes from its crouch, leaping two to four and a half metres from a standing start. It then streaks away, hopping this way and that in a tricky zigzag pattern. This movement makes it very difficult for predators to follow.

Although rabbits and hares are usually silent creatures, all of them are able to let out a terrible, ear-piercing scream when they are captured or in serious danger. This often results in their being quickly dropped by their startled attacker.

A New Bunny Season

Young rabbits and hares just out on their own are in particular danger. They have not yet learned all their parents' escape tricks, and many unwary youngsters will fall prey to a watchful owl or fox.

The rabbit or hare that survives these first difficult weeks will soon be ready to start its own family. With luck, rabbits will live to one or two years of age, and hares may live for three or more years.

Special Words

Buck Male rabbit or hare.

Burrow A hole in the ground dug by an animal to be used as a home.

Courting dance A dance that always follows the same pattern and that is performed by rabbits and hares during the mating season.

Desert Hot dry area with few plants or trees.

Doe Female rabbit or hare.

Fall prey Become a meal for another animal.

Form Hollow in the ground made by a rabbit or hare snuggling in to sleep.

Grooming Brushing or cleaning hair or fur.

Herbivore Animal that eats mainly plants.

Kit Baby rabbit.

Leveret Baby hare.

Lichen A flowerless moss-like plant which grows on rocks and trees.

Litter Group of animal brothers and sisters born together.

Marsh Soft, wet land.

Mate To come together to produce young.

Mating season The time of year during which animals will mate.

Swamp Area where the ground is soaked with water.

Tundra Flat land in the Arctic where no trees grow.

Warren Piece of ground containing many rabbit burrows. European rabbits live in warrens.

INDEX

Cover Photo: William Lowry.

Photo Credits: Valan Photos: page 4 (Wayne Lankinen), 7, 16, 32, 35, 41, 43 (Stephen J. Krasemann), 8, 30, 37 (Brian Milne), 11 (François Morneau), 12 (Albert Kuhnigk), 19 (Kennon Cooke), 20 (Francis Lepine), 23 (J. D. Markou), 24 (Esther Schmidt), 27, 28, 45 (Harold V. Green); David R. Gray: 15, 39.